Slick

Like Dark

Slick
Like Dark

MEG WADE

TUPELO PRESS
T|P *North Adams, Massachusetts*

Library of Congress Cataloging-in-Publication Data available upon request.

ISBN: 978-1-946482-31-0

COVER PHOTO:
Hal Wade. *Untitled.*

*Cover and text designed and composed
in Adobe Caslon by Dede Cummings.*

TUPELO PRESS
P.O. BOX 1767, NORTH ADAMS, MASSACHUSETTS 01247
(413) 664–9611 / editor@tupelopress.org / www.tupelopress.org

Tupelo Press is an award-winning independent literary press that publishes
fine fiction, nonfiction, and poetry in books that are a joy to hold as well as
read. Tupelo Press is a registered 501(c)(3) nonprofit organization, and we rely
on public support to carry out our mission of publishing extraordinary work
that may be outside the realm of the large commercial publishers. Financial
donations are welcome and are tax deductible.

Produced with support from the National Endowment for the Arts

ART WORKS.
arts.gov

Contents

))

I know I have sinned,

but I am paying for it.

Lady of the South

Here lies the dark place in a room

                                        Hear the banjo claw-hammer horror

A waitress   only a girl   then a stranger

                    forced himself inside her

Body flung limp in the basement closet
                                                his hammer no
                        his fists no
                                his palms burnt ribs in defeat shaken
                awake skull bashed against a shelf

        full of peach cans

                                        Imagine this is how you're taught to pray

            Please *[stop]* clawing its way out of a mouth

There's a knot on the back of her head

                                        Blood on her skirt

A lady carries around this darkness until she gets tired

I am so tired.

The Defense

There's a thing in my chest,
            a punch table I'd like to swallow.

                                   I cannot be afraid to tell it all wrong.

Here are the facts:

        I know that I know how to kill   *that makes me an adult.*

             I know I might not leave here with the pardoned letter
                 I hope for, but that the rest will become
        clear in the short time I'm allowed.

So what if I didn't give up
            the ship   let the record show I drew flags
                                      signaling
                            I carried dangerous goods

           —a proper wolf whistle   more leg
                my prowl fearsome as a waitress
waking up from a Blue Ridge wedding lips swollen and twenty-two rounds
gone from the pistol.

When I mentioned the gun just now, what did you imagine my body doing?

Something like dancing, but not dancing?

The farthest point from celebration.

This is what surviving feels like—

The fact is he didn't kill me and now I have a long time left to live.

Clearly, I'm doing the best I can.

I had to take my spoiled body and build lights around it.

Get down on my knees and pray
I'd be visible again.

I witnessed every terrible thing my right hand would show me.

I can only hope to be judged
not by the precision of the barn fire
but by the consequences of my confession.

Half lullaby   half field-holler

I'm not just chewing with my mouth open.

If the saying's true   if you love someone
you should get to know them as best you can   then I have tried—

All that drinking I did that Christmas   blown-out hose and skint knees
            my dress ghosting floor after foreign floor

                    I was just trying to take my body back.

Hallelujah Holler Asylum

1.

Sit still, so I can
                    get the story right.

The storm might blow open the screen door any minute
                    now, the chickens running
                                        wild through the yard

    and there's still so much I need to tell you—

I learned more about sanctuary from nakedness than I have in any cathedral.

                         Folded my hands in prayer too many times to forget
        the deep crushed velvet in the backseat of a stranger's Chrysler, lips
                                        pressed against eyelids
                    lips pressed against everywhere, a stranger's thumb
        in the corner of my eye trying to pop it out

                                        a peeled grape.

—Alright

        so there's a vengeful and a saving God in fucking.

                    That's as good a place to start as any.

2.

There's so much we can't see through fogged windows.

A rowboat on a lake of sewing needles.

My body, a small brave house.

I'm in the kitchen cooking apples when I fold over.

My skin hugs my bones like the two have finally fallen in love.

—Goddamnit, Christ has everything to do with this:

authority of the stripped body   salvation

our necks and how easily they snap.

3.

An old room   a mattress on the floor.

You reading the same book, you
          wearing your first blonde mustache and no shirt

                                        you changing
the light bulb
          again because I'm too short to reach it

                              the school bus full of children
     outside not making anything

                                        better, only louder.

You're not talking but you ask if I can hear you.

          I need to know if God belongs within a body.

                              What kind of question is that?—

4.

Desire is a miracle.   Here, let me show you.

5.

Your knuckles wrinkle together as if they are small
                                                    black rivers
                        pouring into one another.

            Carpenter hands.   *Honey knuckles.*

If the hands are dirty that means they're working,

                                        tender and building
a place where I can love a man again.

Habeas Corpus

Loosen the cuffs   at this point, I think

I deserve to hear some answers   you want me to present

the body   well here it is—

                        smearing mascara all
                        over the cellar walls

Never again will I take   a beating

survive a blurry walk   out of the woods

hollering for mercy like   the whole thicket's on fire

my heart snapping   like a bird's leg

                        go ahead / search me
                        find me / I consent

I have a scar on the inside of   my belly button where

they ripped out what was left of   my broken organ in trouble my small shoulders stowed in the cellar

another man shirtless in cutoffs

to hold myself prisoner

but the truth is

I'm innocent

for weeks haven't let myself see

sweat out the best heat of July

any longer would be foolish

I still don't know whether or not

I'm innocent

I'm innocent

The Skinning House

There's howling in the woods out back.

           That light at the bottom of the pool.

           All my fucking hair in the bathtub.

There are empty spaces inside me and here I am hiding my body
  in broad daylight.

           Tell me, what's romantic about this undoing?

The table of instruments looks
           eager and my chest is so fleshy
                      and human.

If you're going to cut me open   if you're going to get low down

I'm going to wail like you've pulled something out of me—

Arrested Empire

I don't know what I was expecting here:

Cast-iron music?

A bit of gold undressing the piano?

The night filled with the sound of living room songs sung by everyone
I've ever loved and me
smiling so much I'm told to put my teeth away—

Girl　　　　*you're grinning like a butcher's dog.*

Girl　　　　*you got vinyl-shine eyes.*

Instead, I toss rocks at the fried chicken sign to knock the neon out.

If something is beautiful

it's fighting.

This endless war of Spanish moss　　　　kudzu choking
the graveyard's magnolia
and the bees, hundreds of them
trapped in the ceiling of this old house til honey dripped down
the dry-wall

                                                                       homesick for you

          to press your tongue against it.

                  There are so many ways to be trapped.

The farm's abandoned silos, the moon flooding
                the tobacco

                      fields are almost in that category.

Three Dead Stags

float the creek giant

horns locked soft bellies

distended twelve wet

hooves slick like dark

orchids I measure

their antlers they stretch

almost four-hundred

inches of bone I saw

two of the heads off zip

tie the horns I need help

dragging the remaining body

out of the water to assemble

the toothy shadow of what

comes next—I will not know

what to say when you find me

here a symphony of wasps

hovers nearby I focus on six

milky eyes I cannot help

but wonder why the third

latched what battle now lost

the thin needle of forever empties

a soft sound as it pricks I saw

a clump of lights and thought

it was a child I admit I loved

a man so wildly music thinned

each necessary thrum stopped

pulsing I wait along the bank

my heart split into threes these

bloated bodies provide evidence

the forsaken stags the lost hiccup

no we do not always drown alone

Young Cotton

I flood as there is no one left
to swim to—chipped polish

skirt lifted, my soft shoulder
pushed hard against the dead

hemlock tree, please god don't see
anything besides flesh wet purpose

when you float your thirsty
hands around my trusting

neck—I tell you I want them
there—yes—don't stop—

harder—the light finally breaks

when I open my mouth. Hose
ripped in two different places.

A sinful woman washed Christ's feet,
dried them with her hair, imagine

all the ways a pair of country knees
can worship their way home. Witness

the black earth of my eyes, my violent
fanfare, this young cotton all red

stemmed and blanketing the field.
Deliverance begins with the body

and sweeps outward. Please don't
let me go to Heaven alone.

Valley Psalm

Because the base of a mountain loses light   first

      I tried to collect it.

Hold it inside my closed and quiet   lips.

We were young when I decided I wanted to live

           the rest of my days in that small yearning
     country with you.

           Even a blind hog finds an acre every now and then.

Doubt silent as anonymous
         gods at a kitchen table—the days

   an arabesque, a white dress, the meridian of my heart split open,

              floating
     away in separate directions.

If I ever become lost, if you ever lose me, look for me

           in a world where we're all bad
     at geography, and still love

         peaches.

Place your hands on top of my hands like ghosts do
                                                when they're trying
            to get your attention.

Take the crowbar to the pews   who says we need church.

Apologia Attempt

I place my mouth
against the soft lawn

of a boy and touch
something so deep

inside him, it's frightening.

Pure blind alarm.
What do you expect

me to do with that?
Clumsy hands shouldn't

fool with porcelain. Who
wants to love a broken thing—

Yes, I fuck with the devil.

I once made my best
friend so mad she drove

her car with both of us in it
headlong into a hickory

hard enough to knock
the wheels off the axle.

Go ahead, imagine
what I did to hurt her.

Maybe I did deserve it.

There was an instance of blue
china clattering the hardwood

in June, the apothecary bottles
lined up along the window labeled

poison, love, forgiveness, all of them
looking the same, the same

confusing antique scrawl.
It's foolish to believe

we can't contain this kind
of darkness. All night long

the moon can betray herself.

It's no secret, the way
she turns her face

away from the light.

Bleached Acoustics

We left the old swing
unpainted. Cast spoiled

rinds off the porch
for the deer to lick clean

through. All night long
I heard something

crying, and surrendered
myself to the invisible

ropes of smoke left
in its song. My Love,

sometimes we can't
choose what we save.

We just can't choose.

Sometimes, we pull young
lungs from the water

capsized, already drowned.
Were we too soon? Not yet—

I should've let you fuck me,
but instead you watched

me pack. My hands
on the headboard no longer

a steeple, but a bomb. Boom.
One last wave goodbye

in a cornflower dress.
In terms of identifying

guilt, this suitcase is useless,
but I pride myself on being

a woman with a dress
for every occasion

and there's a pocket
in the seam here, a list

of all the things I can carry:
a mirror, a matchbook, my own

muddy voice howling
bleached acoustics.

There are good ones
of us who disappear.

Who pay no attention
to the sign behind the bar

No Sex On The Pool Table.
Too many cigarettes stamped

in the wood grain. This
wrestling beneath our shirts

we hush with our hands.
When I first kissed you

I had a soft, bright heart.
Please remember, I did

not ask for this. I did not
ask to be a reliquary of dark

purpose. My darling, this
is where I leave you like

the greedy little songbird
I am.

Ditch Tender

Say the headlights don't shine
                    through the grain
                              field, tires
            spun, say she only clipped
     the hay bale when she barreled
                    down the road. A life is still a life at eighty
                                        miles an hour, so say
the wheel turned, say you've seen her out there pitching
                         a fit, prick her bare feet black earth, say
            she raised her hands in the air cracking
the band bigger than the radio.

                 Say she clambered out of it.

Say she became something else.
                              A better animal.

                 Bulletproof.
Says she's not better off
            dead than lost, eyes like black eggs, say you saw her rise
     a pistol when she's angry.

Say she won't surrender   here.

Say if she does, you won't   blame her.

Field Notes

1.

I called you from the truck stop.
                              I planned to sleep there
                                          all night

The attendant mumbled something over
                    the loud-speaker about how unattended baggage
          may be suspect, but I was busy talking to you, so I wasn't
                                                paying attention.

          I was too concerned about the caution
                        tape surrounding the entrance.

                              Why must relief need a warning?

I only pulled the car over to unclench my hands in the first place.

2.

You once told me I felt pain so deeply you needed
                              to build a bridge over it, wide
                    enough for us both to stand on—

                    You bought green muck boots.

You became a carpenter.

You told me, "you have to be tough with fruit
trees, don't let them out stay
their welcome."

I uprooted everything.

No more peaches.

3.

Dead bees tangled in my hair means July is almost over.

The rain against the rhododendron
tunnels makes the forest roar and seem impossible
to leave.

You haul the garbage bags full
to the side of the road and we do
terrible things to each other.

How did you picture this ending?

We flip the switch.   The light goes off.

Surely, even the sea forgets its wreckage.

4.

Night flooded and I couldn't find the bridge
                        anymore (was there a bridge).

        The lazy capo of the moon, drunk and forgetting—darkness
doesn't destroy; it only confuses.

        I thought I saw you in the fog, but it was only a stranger
                                standing beside a fence.

            Shadows ambush like evening medications.

    My clumsy hands no longer pointing to the moon, but at the pink ribbon
                                blood makes
                        when it mixes with water and
circles
                                                the
drain.

                Tell me, where is the bridge—

    If this is really what I think this is, then I cannot
                                screw this up.

5.

I climbed into the car.

                Spread

the Atlas across the dashboard.

Look at how much space I'll live
without you.

6.

I unbraided
my long hair in the rearview, every exit sign
a vertebra along the highway's back;

possibility without the bruises.

Sweetheart, I'm ready to confess tomorrow isn't coming for us.

I pulled the car over,
whispered your name
into a shoebox, and abandoned it in the river
where we surrender
the things we long for most.

The empty passenger seat is real and it must no longer depend on you.

I mistake shadows for churches.

I've built a whole world out of lack.

The Ambulance Outside isn't Really A Moving Truck

The medics positioned the gurney and shut the doors. *Is it a gurney or a stretcher?* A structure. I wish it didn't matter I can't see you anymore. It's dark and this old town doesn't believe in streetlamps. The basement floods, so we keep the important boxes on wire racks. The water rises and the little bridges to my heart become impassible. Maybe I'm in the belly of something. *You know what happens to the girl who's swallowed by monsters?* Rescue. Yes, it's the fisherman who finally cuts the thing open, but it's always been up to her to crawl out of the dark.

Almost Refrain

The whole messy thing
unraveled like a horse

belly, split open

and spilled. A wasp
nest, gristled angels,

it's strange, how scared
I am—quick write

down, Ferris wheel.
Write down, ceiling

of bees. Carefully mark
the lover pulseless

in the middle of a very long,
high road we never see

the end of—my throat

falls right out of my body.
A moth's wings before

the dust knocks off.

I Blame The Woods And Keep The Body

A body is dead and I want you to be responsible.

                                        You've seen his hands.

          You know what they were capable of—

My baby, old honey knuckles, building our imagined house.

This could be a place where I would love him like a woman
who wants to have babies would.

Our imagined babies might hold
                              each other's tiny imagined
        hands and go walking through
                        the very real woods together.

  The woods are a dangerous place for an imagined thing

                                    to happen.

Have you been to hell?

An imagined house can be a kind of hell depending
on what the day is like—

depending on whether or not we are all still

alive.

I flooded the house.

There are no children.

I keep his body in the bathtub.

The smell is so terrible I hold my sleeve over my mouth.

I don't want it to end this way.

Perhaps we could be sitting at a real table and I could

       ask him to hand me a real can opener and this could be

   the most exciting part of our day.

      This way no one has to die.

This way, we're just two people lying

    down on opposite sides of the kitchen floor.

Notes

The epigraph at the beginning of this book is from Ai's poem, "Motherhood, 1951" (New York: W.W Norton & Company, 2010).

The line, "I know that I know how to kill, that makes me an adult" is borrowed from Yehuda Amichai's "Wildpeace" in his *Selected Poetry* (Berkeley: University of California Press, 1986).

Acknowledgements

Many thanks to the editors & staff of the following publications in which early versions of these poems have appeared:

CutBank, Banango Street, Horsethief, Linebreak, Nashville Review, New South, Pinwheel, Phantom Books, The Feminist Wire, and *Whiskey Island.*

"Habeas Corpus", "The Skinning House", and "Arrested Empire" appear in *Read Women: An Anthology* (Locked Horn Press, 2014).

So much thanks and gratitude to Kristina Marie Darling, Jeff Levine, and Tupelo Press for bringing this book into the world, and to The University of Wisconsin-Madison and the Diane Middlebrook Poetry Fellowship, without whose support this book would not be possible.

My deepest gratitude to my friends and teachers, Richard Siken and Jane Miller, for their guidance, support, and encouragement of these poems. Your patient teaching and generous hearts allowed my voice to become exactly what it is, and nothing less. I am forever so grateful for you.

Thank you to my forever poetry friends for their careful readings, critiques, and for always championing the betterment of myself and my work: Shelly Taylor, Hannah Ensor, Sarah Minor, Carly Joy Miller, Andrea Francis, Ben Rutherford, Cory Aaland, Sarah Schoenbrun, Nancy Powaga, Justin Yampolsky, Mike Powell, Heather Hamilton, Garrett Faulkner, Jess Langan-Peck, Amaud-Jamal Johnson, Lauren Russell, Tana Welch, Timothy Welch, Caitlin Quinn, Mikey Swanburg, and Kara Candito, Thank you for sharing in or guiding my journey, I am so honored to know you all.

Thank you to my younger brothers: Luke Wade, Davis Paine, and Lee Paine for being the people to make me laugh the most during the writing of this book, and for being my favorite moving company when I had to travel to write it. Thank you to Al Wade and David Paine for all your love.

Thank you to the incredible tribe of Tennessee women who have raised me. Thank you for your unyielding support and love throughout the many years this book took shape: My Mama (Suze Paine), Martha Bryant, Courtney Davis, Kristie Schleicher, Elizabeth Bradley, Caitlin Overstreet, and Anna Phillips. Thank you for your strength and vulnerability and thank you for your tremendous love. My world is made better by having all of you in it.

And finally, lifetimes of gratitude to Ryan William Butz; thank you for turning on the light.

CPSIA information can be obtained
at www.ICGtesting.com
Printed in the USA
JSHW041525120320
4698JS00005B/11

9 781946 482310